Thinking *With* Your...

By Birdie Chesson

Miss Birdie's Books, Inc.
New York

ISBN:
978-0-692-46556-1
Copyright 2017 by Birdie Chesson

All rights reserved. Published by Miss Birdie's Books, Inc. and associated logos are trademarks and/or registered under
Miss Birdie's Books, Inc.

Thinking with your is registered under MBB, Inc.
Printed in the U.S.A.

To Renee

This book is dedicated to us.

Love,

Birdie

Table of Contents

Foreword   6

Introduction: 11
What does it all about?

Dominant   15

Mind Dominant   31

Heart Dominant   48

Getting on the Same Page   68

- Love Facades and
  "The Competition"   84

- Unconditional Love   93

- Ride or Die VS
  For Better or Worse   95

- Soul Ties, Twin Flames &
  Soulmates   100

- The Inner Work and Trauma   108

- Baby Mama Drama and
  Un-Hoeing Yourself   122

Doing the Work   138

Thank You   151

FOREWORD

I wanted to write this book for the daughter that I never birthed, for the young ladies that I have the privilege to know, yet to know and to _you_, one of my sisters in this life. As I always let y'all know, I love you and I want what's best for you. This is for our journey together.

I don't believe in regrets. It makes you stay in the past too long. Whenever you look back, you tend to dwell, then you feel those feelings and 9 times out of 10, it gets you back into trouble. I believe in learning your lessons or you're destined to repeat them. And you stay in the mindset it put you in.

I had to admit that I needed to change how I've treated myself. I am a great person but in the past, I let the _incomplete_ parts of me control _everything_ about me.

Sometimes it was my brain, thinking too much. Sometimes it was my heart, feeling too much. Then sometimes it was *her*, my pussy, that did the deciding for all of us.

Now before you think of this book or even the use of the word *pussy* is me being vulgar, that's fine. Not everyone is going to have the same thinking process or even able to conceive that the prospect even exists. But the reality is, it does. Your pussy is one of your best friends for life. So whatever name you want to call her, substitute it, the message here is absolutely worth it.

In the past, I'd meet someone, thought they were nice but something was off, but I'd still let it go because of the prospect of what it *could be* was bigger than what it actually was. I enjoyed the energy, let my pussy lead and make decisions on the behalf of my heart and mind. I was lying to myself and making decisions that had nothing to do with what I wanted or needed.

I used my pussy to stay in relationships that I knew I should have left. I used my pussy to go further with men than I wanted to. I used my pussy to weigh the pros and cons to fit what I thought I wanted. I was a coward hiding behind my heart and mind, using my pussy. I used my pussy to control my actions and here I was, making heartless and mindless choices, carrying me through drawn out and sometimes torturous situationships, ending up with place holders, space fillers and bookmarks. Did I have to stay this way?
Of course not.

The best part of knowing what we've done gives us the power to shift towards what we really want, giving ourselves the permission to change, especially if you're not happy living that way. There's so much more to life and way much more to love.

I can laugh now when I think about myself within my personal journey to now but the reality at the time was that it wasn't funny at all.

I would've been destined to stay in limbo in my love life unless I got all of **us** on the same page, making the *same* love decisions based on incomplete and/or portions; heart, mind ***and*** pussy.

The roller coaster ride ends here. In the interest of transparency, here I am. Hopefully, pieces of mine and other's journeys can help you in your own self-exploration.

Don't let the title drive you away. Remember the reason you picked the book up in the first place.

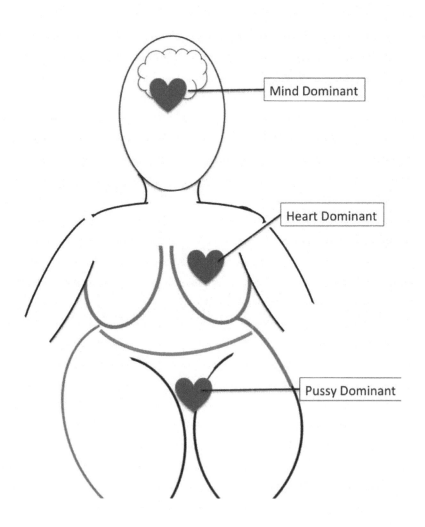

Mind Dominant

Heart Dominant

Pussy Dominant

Thinking *WITH* Your 🐱 : What's it all about?

We are all dominated by parts of who we are. Sometimes you'll explain it away by saying, "That's my personality." "That's how I was raised." Or "I'm a Libra. That's why." There's a whole plethora of excuses and rationalizations that we make up as to why we are how we are and *who* we are.

This book's position is that people deal with things cerebrally, wholeheartedly or reactionary.

This book is all about thinking and feeling with *all of you* in mind. What do I mean?

When you are **Mind Dominant**, you make decisions based on logic or with mental rationale.

Heart Dominant implies that you're dealing in your emotions and feelings.

Pussy Dominant is without thought or emotion, usually impulsive or reacting, using visual or carnal desire.

Being one or the other is not wrong *per say* (if you're happy), but when you are thinking, feeling and seeing with all hands on deck, firing on all barrels you are at an advantage and can master any situation, especially in love. You'll definitely be a happier woman because you are creating how you love and receive love instead of reacting to circumstances you end up in.

The only person that you can control is yourself in any situation. Picture driving a car, <u>YOU</u> control the speed, the direction and can dodge any actions from others that may put you in danger as much as you can because you are aware and can drive defensively.

Life is so unpredictable and when you encounter people on an organic level, you always have the choice of whether to draw them in or shut them out. Period.

When you are seeing with everything you need to see from *all* sides of yourself, you definitely got this.

Now, there is no surefire way to prevent calamity in dealing with other people's human nature, but you definitely have control over how you respond and react with your own.

Sis, you got this.

The Rundown:
Pussy Dominant

It was almost two months after 9/11 and I was still traumatized, like most New Yorkers. The loss of my family member and the trauma from my own near death experience wounds were still fresh. I was just existing at that point and did a lot of self-destructive things to numb the pain. Like the night I met *him*.

A co-worker invited me to his birthday party and I was his guest. I knew he liked me, but I wasn't interested. But after 3 months of moping, I needed to get out of the house and I was guaranteed VIP bottle service at this nightclub, so I stopped sulking and went.

Now, when I accepted my co-worker's invitation, I didn't know it was a Latin club. Music was mostly Salsa and Merengue and I didn't know about dancing to either. I had my drinks and everyone danced. Then, a familiar song came on and I jumped up and hit the floor like a tornado and danced the hell out of that song.

The DJ only played the intro and it lasted literally one minute. A Bachata song came on and I made a B-line back to my seat.

A man grabbed my waist. "Excuse me Miss." I turned around, he smiled his sexy smile. I said, "I'm sorry, I'm not familiar with the songs." He said, "Me neither. And we're the only black people here." I looked around. We both laughed. "Can I get you a drink?" He guided me through the crowd to the bar. I ordered my whiskey sour and he looked at me and said, "That's a strong drink." I blushed. "Well it's what I like." We talked as the party went on without us and before long, the night was over.

He was on his way home with his friends and he gave me a gaze. "Do you want to come home with me? I'll make breakfast."

I'm still a sucker for breakfast in bed.

I jumped into the cab with the sexy stranger and... let's just say that he made me breakfast.

After the night/morning was over. I gave him a number. The wrong number and left. He was my first one night stand and I didn't feel bad about it.

Exactly one month later, I'm crossing the street and who is walking towards me?

The handsome stranger.

He stopped me. "Birdie, I'd really like to see you again. Can I take you out?" I hesitated, knowing I had given him the wrong number with the intention of never seeing him again. "Ok." I said. "Can I get the correct phone number this time?" An awkward laugh came out of me. I put my number in his phone. He instantly called me to verify and he took me on a date 2 days later.

We did dinner and a movie. A movie that we never saw the end to because at the very end, he looked at me, kissed me so passionately that the movie played on without us.

We had to buy the movie when it came out on DVD to see the ending. We spent the rest of the night in a hotel.

We were young and free with no inhibitions, always together and before long, we were in love. I was scared because I never wanted to be in love with Doug or anyone else for that matter. I was hurt in the past by my first boyfriend years back. I just wanted to have fun and sing. Doug was carefree like me and I wanted to ride the wave of euphoria.

I found out that Doug was in a relationship when we met. I pieced it together after he said that his ex was angry and stalking him because of the way things ended between them. It bothered me and I was upset about it but we were already several months in and he kept reassuring me that they were "over". And as far I was concerned he was "free". *Not my problem, right?* Humph.

Yeah right. Don't ignore those things. It will be your problem if you don't approach it head on.

As a singer in a band, we were building momentum, booking gigs left and right. I loved it. Doug went to every show and wore a suit very nicely, accompanied me to industry cocktail parties and could hold a great conversation. "Hmm, I'm on the rise, I think he's someone I can take on my journey." As I started to think future with Doug. We talked about marriage and even looked at rings. Priced them and even designed the idea of them.

On our 2nd anniversary, we met in a hotel. I was there first and heard a knock on the door. I looked through the peephole. All I saw were roses. I knew it was Doug, he was funny that way.

I opened the door and he presented the two rings that we had designed. One for him and one for me. It was a sweet gesture and we were content. After putting the rings on, we dressed up, went on a boat cruise in the middle of the harbor.

We moved in together shortly thereafter in our first apartment and everything flowed seamlessly.

Then I got pregnant. I couldn't work in clubs anymore and got less singing gigs. I was in college and worked as an electrician during the days. After awhile, I couldn't work anymore. Apart from school, I was stuck in the house and Doug was still going out with his friends and after awhile, he started coming home less and less.

Excuses were doing double shifts to get ready for the baby. Then it was his sick mother. I was feeling like a caged bird. In my gut, I knew there were other people. I was so turned off, that I didn't want him to touch me. I had our son, Bam. He was born with a cleft palate and needed surgeries and therapies. The overwhelming guilt and postpartum left me paralyzed. I wanted to get out of this toxic relationship but I didn't know how.

After telling him how lonely I felt and he reassured me that he wasn't cheating, I let his words soothe me. He was now more attentive and romantic like he had been before. He came home from work, put the baby to sleep, rubbed my feet and catered to me. Just because, he'd make dinner, spread rose petals on the bed. Breakfast in bed. My head was at peace.

One morning, he jumped in the shower before work and I started laundry. He had emptied his pockets on the table and there they were: 2 movie tickets and a receipt to a famous seafood restaurant. Livid wasn't the word. Enraged was more like it. I rifled through his gym bag, found a card with a woman professing her love for him. When he got out of the bathroom, I showed him the card. He had that blank look in his eyes. "You're the one that got me."

I said, "This is the prize? You?"

He went to work and I went digging some more. Bank statements with several purchases at a known baby store and it wasn't for Bam.

He didn't come home that night.
I was stewing.

When he came home that Sunday night, he took a quiet shower and slid into the bed.

I couldn't sleep but I couldn't turn over.

"She's pregnant." He whispered in his sleep. "She's pregnant?" I screamed. I started to beat his chest. He sat up and sobbed. "I'm so sorry." As he pleaded for my forgiveness, Bam woke up.

My ears were so hot. I didn't know what to do with myself.

Later, I spoke to his mother. "Stay with him, that's what a real woman does. He's a man."

I spoke to my father, who was in hospice at the time. "Stay with him. He's just scared. Fatherhood is new, he'll grow out of it."

"I don't want to do this anymore, Dad. I'm still young and I don't want to live this way."

"Just give it time." My Dad said.
I stayed. The baby was born and he came home as usual. He had his routine that was all about me and Bam. One day, I looked at him, "When are you going to see your child?"

He was stunned. As upset as I was, I definitely didn't want him to be a deadbeat dad with his new son. So he'd go over to see him on Saturdays after his football league. He emptied his pockets on the kitchen table like he used to and took his shower. And there they were again, movie tickets.

I waited for him to get out of the shower. I screamed. "Why are you going to the movies? The baby is a newborn. This is a date!" He looked at me with his blank look. I tossed his clothes in the wash, stewing.

I was done. I sat on the couch, waiting for the clothes to get dried. I looked at his keys on the table. Took one of my electrical tools and cut the keys in half, one by one.

I stayed up all night. He woke up to get ready for work that Friday. I made him breakfast to go. As I ushered him out of the door, I watched him get on the elevator and watched him make his way down the street towards the train. I stuck close to the window for 10 minutes in case he needed to come back for anything. I called him to make sure he was on the train, asking if he was going to go out after work. He told me that he was coming home after work and that he loved me.

Too little, too late. I packed all of his clothes, cups, gifts, toothbrush; everything that belonged to him. My sister came and we loaded everything into her car and drove to his mother's house. She opened the door and emptied the suitcases on the guest room bed. "He's your problem now." I said to her.

Went to my sister's house that evening and he made countless calls that night. His messages were all fluctuating between, please don't leave him, to why am I leaving to and vowing that he would change, then angry about the keys.

But after all of this, I believed in patterns and unchanged behavior, not his words. Insanity by definition is thinking that the same patterns would have a different result. Why would his behavior have to change? He was who he was, so why would things change? Because of *my* expectations? The only person that I can change is me. Then everything else has the ripple effect of my actions or inaction. By the time my change occurred, the circumstances between us were beyond repair.

"This is how men are." Those words from my father and his mother echoed in my mind. That thinking isn't unique, there's a whole, "All men are dogs" ideology that has spanned generations.

No. This is not how men are. Men take care of their women, mentally, emotionally as well as providing protection and security.

I hadn't felt secure and protected in so long, being on the raw edge of sadness, I had nothing else left to give.

Bam and his therapies, work and school was all I had energy for. No more toxic madness. Doug was so angry that I had 'abandoned him' that he didn't talk to me, not even for our son's sake, for many years.

Since he couldn't get his way anymore, I also was now a single mother. For the record, a Single Mother means (not implies) that the parenting was **_solely mine_** (health, education, life & death decisions, extra curricular; etc.) while he was in his feelings about us. No us? Not even a father's presence in our son's life for a long time. (Not a bash, pure truth). That relationship took years to re-cultivate, reinstitute with new norms established. Sometimes it's like that.

My story isn't unique. There are several single mothers out there that are recovering from love lost. Whether or not there's bitterness on her end or his end. The children suffer. So it's so important to re-establish new terms in reference to the children, then redefine the co-parenting agreement.

That's a different conversation for a different book.

Yes, I could've handled things in a different way. But regardless of public opinion and the peanut gallery, I did what I could to maintain my own sanity and I couldn't consider his feelings anymore. It's that simple.

Self-preservation. That's how it has to be sometimes. The manipulation and narcissistic behavior was mentally abusive and a lot of times, family and friends don't want to believe that of their friend, favorite cousin, brother or nephew are capable of that behavior. It is what it is. People take sides because the devastated parties over-share. The toxicity spreads like a wildfire, causing conflict, divisions and does damage for years.

Since I don't believe in living with regrets, here are some words for the future that I'll expand on later:

1. If you feel that something is wrong in your relationship, listen to yourself.

2. Make decisions that you are comfortable with and stick to them. Don't waver.

3. There will always be differences between you and your chosen partner, but if those differences takes you somewhere that you feel like you're losing the best of yourself, leave that person alone. It won't get better.

If there's no reason to change, no accountability, why would someone change? You have to be the change.
You deserve peace of mind and only you can give that to yourself. Sometimes it takes your mind to get you out of situations that your pussy put you in. Learn from it and heal your heart.

MIND DOMINANT –

Good on Paper

After my relationship with my son's father Doug, I said to myself, never again. I had given way too much. It was my second heartbreak, but it was the one that made me the defensive driver in my relationships thereafter.

Reeling from the hurt from the cheating and the lies, I said that my heart was off the table. If I wanted someone in my future, he'd have to be good on paper. Someone who was doing better than I was. I started analyzing my feelings in my head instead of feeling the actual feelings. I was determined to stay in my head instead of giving my heart.

I became a total contradiction inside of what I wanted to present myself as. On the outside, I was still a bubbly, cheerful and optimistic person. But inside, I was sad, insecure, mourning love and feeling hopeless.

And while I wasn't a complete phony, I was so blindingly optimistic about my future, life and love, that I didn't know where the hurt and the hope started and ended.

When I met Melvin, he looked good on paper. Mel was an older man. A successful corporate maven, smart, very handsome and had social connections. He loved to cook and had a mind that I could go toe-to-toe with, that challenged me intellectually and just like I, he didn't want any more children.

I already had Bam, who was 4 at the time and Mel's children were grown.

We met during one of my favorite pastimes, karaoke. It was a private party and we were both friends of the hosts. Mel couldn't sing to save his life but he was so cute and him singing the song was funny. He saw me, bought me a drink and we even sang a song together.

After the party, I didn't think anymore about it, but he got my number from one of the hosts and when we talked it was a great conversation. We went out for coffee and it turned into dinner, which turned into drinks. We decided that we'd see each other again.

I liked the flow between us because he engaged my mind, which was a nice relief from what I had just gotten out of with Doug 2 years before and he was not rushing me into a sexual relationship.

We always met over coffee during his lunch and before I picked my son up from school. We went according to my schedule because since my son's father and I were still not on the same page and Bam was with me all of the time, except for school, some alternate weekends when I got a break or if I was able to get a babysitter for a few hours.

When we started dating officially, we still took it slow, which I loved because there was no pressure on me.

He always bragged about knowing the owners, chefs and cooks of the restaurants we went to and took pride in showing me the gourmet versions of the restaurant industry.

He bought me clothes from designers that he was familiar with. He had a certain standard for what he wanted me to look like around his friends. It was different for me but I didn't pay it any mind and didn't take it personal because instead of flatly rejecting my wardrobe, he bought me clothes with my size, flattering colors, texture and prints in mind.

When he finally met my son, he was impressed with how smart and his personality was of child-like innocence and sharp wit.

We never rushed into sex because we matched wits mentally, not emotionally or even sexually.

But months later, when we finally did have sex, it was awkward and not pleasurable at all. I thought that he wasn't sexually attracted to me or it was because I was out of practice or not experienced enough.

I was in my early 30's and he was in his 50's. He was very energetic and physically fit but sexually, I was trying to lean in to him but he was pulling away.

I didn't realize that he was hiding an erectile dysfunction because of a hidden heart condition. It actually hurt him to physically have sex. One time, we stopped and he finally told me, I didn't know how to feel about it and much as he tried to make me happy in that way, but we just weren't sexually compatible.

As we spoke about the future and getting married, I said to myself that it wasn't important, because that wasn't what our connection was all about anyway.

We made up with it by making plans, going places and we even talked about my corporate structure as an entrepreneur. He was so smart and strategic, I wanted to pick his brain and use his expertise.

When we went to a children's book signing, he looked at me and said, "You should be doing this."

I already had written 9 children's stories and was stuck on what to do with them because I wasn't an illustrator and I knew that that was what my stories were missing.

Inspired, that week, I wrote my second series of books, and kept the illustrations to simple shapes, circles and squares. I was on a roll!

My mom came over for a dinner party that we were hosting and it began to snow.

Because the El (outside train) tracks had ice on them, public transportation's service was suspended. Being that I lived so far, everyone stayed snowed in. We ate, watched movies and when we all went to bed, my mom pulled me aside and told me that she didn't like him for me.

She said that he had a "God complex". I wanted to understand where she was coming from because I thought that it was because of their ages, my mom being only a few years older than he was. She said that he was self-involved, didn't treat me well and would be selfish as time went on between us.

He and I were talking future and I didn't want my mom to not give us her blessing. But I was an adult, able to make my own decisions, I respected her opinion but decided to move forward with him anyway.

A month later came New Year's Eve, which is my absolute favorite holiday and I was supposed to meet his parents and his children at their annual party at their house in Cape Cod and he asked me what I was wearing. I showed him 2 dresses. He said nothing. I didn't think anything of it until the day that we were supposed to leave and I couldn't reach him. I didn't hear from him for 2 days.

I was devastated. I have a thing about being stood up. My time is valuable, no matter who you are and it's one of the most selfish and inconsiderate things someone can do, apart from secondhand smoke (but I digress). Excuses flooded my mind. "Maybe something happened to him or his parents or his children." That was the only rationale that I could give because we were doing so well, so I thought.

He said that he felt bad after work, laid down and didn't wake up until late. I said that he could've called me at any time, it was New Years but apart from that, I didn't hear from him for 2 days?

He came over with flowers, said sorry. Then he said, "I didn't think that it was really important."

WHOA! After me telling you that it was my favorite holiday, you decided that it wasn't really important? *'Say what you mean and mean what you say'* is one of my principles that I live by and I definitely take you at your word and actions. I didn't say much after the New Years debacle but his words snapped me out of being blindly pro-Mel.

I began paying attention to the things he said and did. I began taking notes. I watched as he'd criticize my clothing. I remembered when in a separate conversation when he mentioned that he hated the dresses that I were deciding on wearing for New Years.

I listened as he would ask why Bam was always with us, a subtly hinted that he didn't sign up to be a father again. In that, I noted that he was beginning to act as if having my son around was a handicap to do what he wanted to do socially or even in the way.

When it began getting hot, he mentioned the Hamptons, Cape Cod, food festivals were all his seasonal go-tos and it wasn't kid-friendly.

Then he started mentioning his ex-girlfriends and how they'd drop off their children at their grandparents' houses for days and weeks on end, meaning that these women had children that were never around.

I was definitely not that kind of mother. I wanted my son around and thought that he liked my son and saw a future with *us*. He said that he wanted me to be his wife but thought that he and I should be alone together more.

I enjoyed his company too but our connection wasn't exactly sexual but it was clear that he thought that my son was in the way, that he wanted me, not my son.

We're a package deal. My son wasn't going anywhere.

Then the last straw was one Saturday morning, as my son watched cartoons that I overheard him tell my son, not to talk to him until he had his coffee. Ever.

The tone of his voice was that of disgust or bother that I wasn't going stand for it. Although my son was young and didn't think anything of it, I felt it. I definitely wouldn't let him project his selfishness on my son.

So I told him to leave and that I didn't want to see him anymore.

He told me that he loved me and didn't want it to be over. But I knew that he was only good on paper and definitely not good for me.

When we met, I thought of a smart man, successful in his field, cultured and could show me things that I didn't know. But he was a selfish man, was not considerate or kind. He wasn't interested in what I wanted or needed as a woman. I deserved more.

When we take our emotions and impulses out of the equation, what do we have? A person that seems good on paper or in my mind with nothing to truly stimulate me long-term. Someone who couldn't nurture all of the parts of what it means for me to be a healthy, well-loved woman and be able to evolve into a better version of myself.

I took our conversations about the future, the culture he introduced to me to as it being something to offer me. The reciprocity to meet him equally was where I thought it would be us in the future was substantial enough for us to try to build a future around.

I've seen relationships, especially old-school relationships that are built on function and what others can provide for you. And after being fearful of another heartbreak, it sounded good to me. Love was not a part of this equation, our relationship was devoid of any true emotion because what he gave me didn't evoke it. There was nothing passionate between us.

It didn't occur to me that I was settling and I wanted to forget my heart and you can't do that to yourself. If I would've stayed with Melvin, I would have been giving up my best years as a mother for a man that wouldn't have loved the best of me.

I pride myself on being a great mom. Holding on to him for the sake of being a man's wife would've been detrimental to my son and I.

There are women that do it all of the time. They choose love over whatever is important to her (family, career, you name it, fill in the blank.)

But sometimes the realization of what it truly costs you doesn't set in until later.

I could've been a willing participant because of what it symbolized. Status, business support and culture. Stability. And I could be in a relationship without giving more of myself than was emotionally possible because it felt safe.

Besides my motherhood, which is everything to me, I didn't realize how much of *myself* that I would actually be compromising in that partnership. I was even settling into a role that definitely wasn't for me physically.

I was on the road to not being satisfied emotionally and sexually because he could only meet me mentally and I where I was afraid to go emotionally. I was oblivious to the fact that in becoming his wife would make me sacrifice my libido. For what?

It would never be balanced for me.

As young girls, we are taught that to have someone, we have to give something up of ourselves.

We find someone and fall in love, only we have something in us that's not enough.

For Melvin, my clothing wasn't good enough, having my son all of the time wasn't good enough and because of his libido, our sex was never enough.

Because we can't see it clearly at the time, we internalize it, never asking ourselves what's *his* problem?

Some men have an idea of or have an ideal woman. I can't tell you how many times that I have heard that I remind a man of a current girlfriend or an ex saying, *"She reminds me of you."* Yeah, Ok. But she's not me.

Mel said that I was the perfect woman. With him, I still felt like was not enough.

Perhaps I was a prototype of his idea of the woman that put her kid on a shelf and had everything else that encompassed his ideal woman. Or that I was the perfect woman **but**... _____ fill in those blanks. I wasn't going to wreck my brain trying to figure it out. It needed to be over. So it was.

The Breakdown:
Heart Dominant

Then came James. It was five months after ending things with Mel and the last day of school for my son for that school year. James was a teacher at my son's afterschool program.

We had made eye contact and made flirtatious comments previously in passing but nothing transpired until that day. My son was glued to James' side, which was rare because Bam wasn't close to any man and his father and I were still not even communicating. It was like I saw him again for the first time.

Before I left the school, James asked me out on a date and it started out to be the best summer I had in a very long time.

He was so kind, generous and cared for my son. He was patient and listened to me, which was refreshing. He was handsome and charismatic. His kisses were intense and passionate, I hadn't felt so loved in so long that even after our first date, I knew that I wanted him to be in my life forever.

My son loved him and the 3 of us went everywhere together, so I thought, "FINALLY! Someone I can really start a future with."

Although he was 10 years younger than I, he was mature and had detailed plans for his future that impressed me. There's nothing like a confident man that knows what he wants. The problem was that as time went on, he also wanted kids with me and I was past that stage in my life and did not want to start over with a baby.

I had always counted out having another baby because Bam was born with a cleft palate and doctors always told me that the chances of having another baby with any birth defects were high. Bam had already suffered so much in his life with therapies and surgeries that the finality in my decision was not hard. I meant it and couldn't be swayed.

James loved me and wanted us to start our life together and that included kids. One of the things that he loved about me was being Bam's mother, and because he loved how I was raising my son and said that he knew that I'd be great to have and build a family with.

Soon, he started to take my decision about children personally and began to resent me. To him, my refusal was a rejection for our growth together. He'd say, "No matter what happened with our family, even having another baby with health issues, we could get through it."

To him, I was making excuses, not really wanting to be with him. Beyond the love that we had, because of the stalemate, we didn't have future intentions for each other. I felt bad because he was still young and deserved children. We went on for a few more months, but in conflict because we were very loving and passionate with each other but it always came back to the baby topic.

After another baby-related disagreement, he left my house upset and I couldn't reach him. It was shortly after then that I found out that he cheated with his college sweetheart. When I found out, I was so hurt by the betrayal.

I was angry but I also blamed myself because I knew that I was holding him up from living his life the way that he wanted in such an important way. But how could we realistically be together? Should I ask him to stop wanting something that was so important to him? I knew the truth so I left him alone.

He still worked at Bam's school so I still saw him every day. We weren't speaking but both of us were still hurting.

After years of conflict, Bam's Dad and I *finally* came to a visitation agreement and Bam went to be with him for his Christmas break. I wanted to live my life doing what I wanted to for myself and my businesses, so I focused on writing more books and music. In December, I released my first music EP, Scandal and after he heard the music, James appeared on my doorstep with flowers on Christmas Eve.

In listening, he knew that he was the inspiration of some of the songs and was moved by the words. I melted as he held me and kissed me so passionately. He wanted to come back to me but we knew that we'd still face the same issues as a couple. There had to be a compromise somewhere.

I was still hurt about his deception but I had to think about it. I didn't like what he did, but he was right.

I had to emotionally distance myself from what happened. A lot of women don't acknowledge that men have feelings about how love is developed and how a future could evolve. When men care, they dissect all of the components in how they see themselves with a woman.

In the push-pull limbo of that relationship
we risked turning into a *situationship,*
which is when a toxic situation develops,
dominates and then dictates the course of
the relationship, and NOW how they relate
to each other. The trust record is broken and
it's never the same, the replay becomes
deafening.

It also made me realize that sometimes we
women settle on being with men with no
intentions because we ourselves don't have
intentions.

We like, care and eventually love someone
but can you actually *grow* together? Can you
make compromises that don't block yours or
your partners' goals or could potentially
stand in the way of either of your happiness?

If nothing substantial is built on a strong
foundation with building and prints to grow,
growth won't happen. It can't.

Limbo sucks for anyone wanting a future. Ultimately, I realized that I was the one with no intentions with him and in his future of us. He knew it. I was the one that was the hold up.

It didn't dawn on me that it was because I wasn't loving with *all of me* with him, that he couldn't see a future *with* me anymore. It didn't matter how much he loved me, he eventually had to move on. That's when he cheated.

When we get hurt and don't move forward in relationships, we have to ask ourselves what is our portion? I could point my finger at him and say "He cheated on me.", but what about my part? People are responsible for their own actions but for every action, (or inaction), there is a consequence. Love isn't enough.

Some men don't *say* what they want. Hell, some of them don't *know* what they want. But there are also men that *do know* and don't want to be in limbo.

If they don't think they're going somewhere in life, they move on or risk being stuck. Being with someone you love wasn't enough. It never is.

I believe that there's a window. A window in love where a man gives up and a future/commitment with her just won't happen.

Sometimes we think that talking him into it will convince him to stay. But what are we convincing him to stay to? Your great and glowing personality?

Then a lot of times we're trying to use our pussy power to keep him. That is not fair and half the time he'll entertain it until it's clear that that offering isn't working. The situation is not being dealt with, it's just being covered up with sex. It can't last for long. It's just prolonging the inevitable. He's going to leave again (mentally, emotionally and eventually physically) and your feelings will be hurt even more.

When using pussy power as a last resort, we end up using that type of power to fit a square peg in a round hole. It draws out a situation that is unwinnable for all involved and makes men and women string each other along with no real future in sight. It changes the dynamic in your relationship to carnal for the sake of connection but it's futile in the long term.

So now he's moved on to the next woman and the woman he once loved in the past is now a liability to his new future.
That's the truth. That's why there's "***the ex***", the one that's hovering like a dark cloud in the background of the new relationship. It's also why some men get married right away after being in a long-term relationship.

If he's self-aware, he'll know what he wants and he's looking for it. If he can't find it in you, in more cases than none, he'll find it in someone else and you'll still be looking for answers in wondering why he didn't pick you.

Since James and I knew that we weren't finished with "being together" and we didn't want to fall within destructive patterns that would hurt each other by being deceptive, we agreed to put all of our cards on the table with an open relationship arrangement. So now we would still be together and now on terms that we were comfortable with.

An open relationship is not a popular concept that many talk about and it's DEFINITELY not for everybody.

This is not everyone's answer.
For the record, there are certain mental detachments and an emotional inner security that has to take place, a letting go of traditional conventions and not caring about how others view your life (if others are aware). Communication and clarity is key between partners.

It's also a situation that people can feel like they're sharing someone if they're not cognizant of the full implications.

"Comparison is the killer of all joy."
If you focus on what you *think* is happening
in 'the other person's relationship', it will
undermine everything you have in your own,
and that goes for everything. It's literally
none of your business, which is why open
relationships aren't for everybody.

For the first time in a long time, I was
happy again. Contrary to what people may
think about open relationships, I didn't feel
like I was settling because I was emotionally
secure with myself and I was comfortable
with where I was with James. I was working
on myself and focused on enjoying my life. I
felt free with **our** version of commitment.

We communicated and if we chose to be with
other people while we were together, all
parties involved were aware of each other.
I didn't ask about his other relationships
and he didn't ask about mine. We were
enjoying where **we** were.

The open arrangement concept was new to me and the choice was made out of our wanting to still be together but not having the commit of forever, depriving him of children. Again, I don't recommend open relationships to anyone not ready for all of it.

We still were *"Netflix and Chillin"*, going on dates and loving on each other. We didn't want to be apart but we could never have a long-term future. I was focused on the future I was building for Bam and I. SinceI didn't want to confuse my son, so other than school and extra special events, Bam didn't see James like before.

We would still have great getaways, great conversations, dinners and movie dates like we never stopped, right where we left off, literally.

We kept confusing ourselves with what we actually were because we still loved each other but we lied to ourselves about the truth of what we really became.

I wanted to enjoy being with him but I also didn't want to delude myself in to wanting more and going back to square one with what we couldn't have. In fact, I became so cerebral at times that I forgot to feel. During a heated discussion, James called me a fake. At the time, it upset me, but in retrospect, I see why he felt that way now.

Even in our new arrangement, we were still back in our relationship. I was the same me, afraid of taking risks. Afraid to go beyond physical into something real. He felt it.

If you don't feel love, you definitely can't show it. You being present doesn't mean a thing. I was just present, acting like I deserved his love just because I was still in it.

Loving for real and not worrying about future events that may have never even happened. To him, I rejected his future with me so I was actually rejecting him. I thought it was drastic but was it really far-fetched? His truth was his truth & I couldn't deny it.

What I was giving was Fear Love, but I wanted to be fearless in love and didn't know how. When men and women suppress their feelings, they deprive ourselves from evolving.

Society has women thinking that we're crazy and emotional. We shouldn't have to crash and burn to discover and be ourselves. But that fear of giving in, gets to be just as bad.

Being with James, I knew how it felt to be adored and deeply loved. When I lost myself in fear, I shoved down how I truly felt and it killed our relationship.

I wanted to be fearless and love him but _how_ to truly love him was lost in translation, my love language didn't seem authentic. I was a fake.

We are *"bright and shiny"* when attract that person. Then a lot of us subconsciously dim our light and fade. Why? Because we don't know how to love ourselves while loving someone else at the same time.

Meanwhile, he's still looking for that same light that drew him to you in the first place and he can't find it so the contrast in our relationships begin. We aren't the same women. It's like a bait and switch.

Eventually, James found it somewhere else. Somewhere familiar. I won't ever excuse cheating, but that's what happened. Ultimately, I couldn't blame anyone but myself. Still afraid to lose, I "yessed" things that I shouldn't have.

So I chose to use this open arrangement as an opportunity to get my "needs" met, while working on myself. I needed to get my mind and heart on the same page as the rest of myself. I had in effect, turned my heart dominant relationship into a pussy dominant relationship.

We tend to have a pre-defined way of how we think love is supposed to be. The truth was that I really wasn't ready for love and I wasn't being truthful about what I had done to myself and to him.

All I ended up doing was pivoting into settling in a relationship that was defined by circumstances instead of cutting my losses and letting go. In holding on, we end up doing more damage.

I was supposed to grieve not lost love, but for the lost me. In not dealing with my past, I was so disjointed and loving with pieces of myself, truly afraid to love as a complete and whole me. We get lost when we think too much, we end up not feeling enough. Then we misuse our pussies, thinking that's the language that men will understand and wonder why we lose.

If you're with a partner whose love and leadership can help encourage that light as you find that balance, that's the best. Having the trusting safety in the partner that brings out the best in you is how you know that's "your person". That security has to come from within their own sense of self.

But sometimes people don't know how to distinguish what's happening in their partner and can't fix it, so they react out of survival and cheat (or do something else destructive.)

It was me. It had to be me. I had to stay in that power in me drew him to my flame. In his anger and frustration with me, he withdrew. That ended up being the best thing that he could've done for me.

I had to decide that I was worth shining my light at all times, be fearless in my love and not be afraid of the future.

I had to create a self that I deemed worthy of a lasting future. There was a beauty in my clarity. No more misguided desire and pussy decisions.

There's a belief that we date at the level of our self-esteem. It's true. How far we decide to go in love has everything to do with us. Not on him. We set the standard.

It was like training wheels on a bike, I wasn't ready to step out on my own. I learned so much about myself in the roller coaster with James. The up and down monotony of each of us wanting a future that wasn't on the docket. I didn't see that it tore him apart.

He really loved me and I treated us like it was what he wanted. Since I set the standard and redefined the terms, he took the reins and steered our journey.

We teach a man how to treat us, then we let him lead. What we allow, is where he'll maneuver. Where James ended up leading us was to a dead end. There was nothing left for either of us. James was not my person anymore.

I knew that I had to get ALL of myself on board within myself if I was going to actually enjoy a full exchange of love, with no fears and with a future partner that I fit what I needed as well as having his needs met.

The prolonged ending of relationships is like booking two destinations to paradise that aren't the same. It was insanity. Expecting long-term happiness from day-to-day marathon with no real landing in sight. There was no way to get to where we wanted to go.

It wasn't fair to him to settle either. Having just pieces of ourselves and unable to enjoy the "all in" of being in an equitable give and take that would grow into something better was off the table. We had to treat it for what it was now. Not in the past of what it could've been nor deluded potential of what it could be.

I needed an exit strategy and it had to be cold turkey. No more holding on.

Getting on the Same Page: Thinking *With* Your Pussy

This whole concept of *Thinking With Your Pussy*, comes from being in the same place of a ***full self-love*** that can't be messed with. A self-love that isn't conditional on having a relationship with anyone else outside of yourself.

When I came up with this book, I thought of the book that I would write for my daughter if I had one. Being honest about the things that I learned about life, love and most importantly about myself within it all.

I would want her to never be ashamed of her past choices, but rather to learn from them.

I would want my daughter to love herself to know that when it doesn't feel right, to leave. No explanations, no excuses. Literally turn around and leave. I would want her to know how it feels to be treasured so that she wouldn't settle for less from anyone, no matter how she felt about them.

Some girls don't grow up with a healthy love from a male father figure and when they grow up, they don't know how to find it from a place of being full of love. Now she's loving from a place of filling a void from what she feels is missing.

When you're searching for love from that void, how can you find it with nothing to compare from? How can you even tell what that love would feel/look like from a love that never existed? You can't. All we have to go on is what we feel on the inside. Or have an idea about, but nothing substantial. We don't want to be led by anyone else's version of their love theories, but to find our own defined version.

There's a lie in our current society that tells our girls that there isn't enough love out there for her, that somehow she isn't enough and that there's a constant audition/competition with other women for her to prove her worth.

Problem is, most of the time, the people causing the competition and setting up the field for "auditioning" aren't even worth the platform that they themselves stand on. And the competition isn't even real.

There's more than enough love to go around. Once you truly understand:

1. Who you truly are as a woman.
2. What you want as a woman and
3. What you want in a partner,

you will work on yourself to be the woman that you need to be, in order to have who and what you want.

Be patient with yourself and do the work for yourself and not anyone else.

When your heart, mind, soul and spirit are on the same page, you look at life and love in a whole different way. The people that we are attracted to and are attracted to us start to change because we've changed what we prefer based on new criteria. We think and feel with more intuitiveness because we don't want to waste our time or feel unsafe.

You become intentional because you're clear on who you are, learned what you want in a partner and confidently and consistently stick with it.

WOMEN CREATE THE STANDARD & SET THE TONE. YOU. ME. WE. **WOMEN CREATE THE STANDARD.** Don't **EVER** forget that.

We see it with what's popular, "the glam girls" vs. "real women", which is the most damaging divide/false narrative/fake competition there is. Society has women judging each other through the eyes of their insecurities and pointing fingers at the lowered standard that men choose us from.

WOMEN CREATE THE STANDARD. Change the narrative and decide how you want to be loved. It has NOTHING to do with how you look or who you think is your *"competition"*. (Again, there is no competition.)

WOMEN CREATE THE STANDARD when we teach our sons about the kinds of women that would benefit him in the long term as they look at the whole picture.

Teach your sons that there is nothing casual about connections. Teach your son to see if this woman loves herself. Can she create a great home life? What are her future plans? What are her intentions with your son? What are your son's intentions with her?

Teach him to be responsible with her heart. Discourage destructive behaviors by holding your sons accountable and letting them know that they're wrong when their wrong, instead making excuses for them.

You setting the standard for your sons to look to within these situations can be the deciding factor for either a stereotypical or a successful connection that will impact generations to come and contributes to your legacy as a mother.

Either way, YOU are setting the standard as the teacher, whether it's you teaching your sons or showing the man you love, how to love you through your own love language. Do you see how important you are to the equation? It's YOU. Remember that.

When we love ourselves as the people we're growing into, nothing can change our focus and ideals. Our connecting with people that bring us down won't happen. People that only like some *parts of us* but not *all of us*, at the sake of what's important to us, can't happen. OUR STANDARD won't allow it.

There is an overtone in society that there are too many women out there and not enough men. Now we're subconsciously watering down a woman's value, which gets diminished and the qualities in her that held her value are now reduced due to petty competitions and putting up with low caliber partners out of her fear of being alone.

First of all, being alone is underrated and alone is often confused with being lonely.

If you have a healthy relationship with yourself, being with someone physically or not won't matter. You can choose *who* you want to be around, *the way* you spend time with them and *when* you choose to because *you've* set the standard.

Loneliness happens when there are things that we don't address within *ourselves*, or things we don't want to 'be alone with', so you find every reason in the world to not be alone, even settling for subpar company.

Perspective: If you don't want to be alone with yourself, how can you expect others to want to be around you? Who are you in reference to others? How can you expect to have a quality connection with someone special if you don't find out who you are and what you truly want?

There's nothing wrong with being 'the life of the party' but the party has to be over at some point. You have to enjoy your own company in order to have an authentic, quality experience with others.

As you evolve and 'clean up' your own vibe, the quantity of people around us dwindles down. When the inner work is done, the people that you spend the most time with may even change. Empowered, you can be picky based on your own criteria: Quality vs. Quantity.

Some people resist change because they are used to their life as-is, whether they love their life or not. Comfortable with being uncomfortable or complacent with how their life is because they can function in the dysfunction and they can manage it, day in, day out. Why change what you can 'deal' with?

Have you ever seen someone so unhappy all of the time? They're so miserable that it's their natural disposition. "Oh that's just who they are." "That's such a _insert zodiac sign_ trait." "She had it hard growing up." "She's cool once you get to know her."

Making excuses or putting up with 'bad behavior' or settling to be around sad people is not what you should be subjecting yourself to. Want more, do more, have and be more. You can't do that, if you're with people that don't want more too.

Someone's personality dictates the things that they think, do and say. And it always dictates their personal reality.
"Personality equals your Personal Reality"

Don't be fooled by someone's presentation if it's filled with inconsistencies. Look at their personal reality, watch what they say and do, because it always reveals how they think. ALL of it is their inner philosophy and eventually, how they'll treat you. Take off the rose colored glasses. If it doesn't add up, Run. Seriously.

It's Ok if you were with someone and change your mind with someone. You have every right to change your life at any point if you're not happy. If what someone has done is inexcusable, why stick around? If you don't like or want to put up with something, why should you?

A quality life begins with quality connections. You don't get that with settling for people that don't fit your standard of living.

There's a saying, if you hang out with 4 idiots, you'll be the 5th idiot. We tell our kids that, we believe in that with money and business, so why not hold yourself to the same standard in love?

That includes just starting out. If you start dating someone and something makes you decide to not call back, don't ghost. Just go.

Ghosting is when you disappear and then you 'float back' and forth into their life. It's cruel and sociopathic. Don't do that. Make a decision and stick with it. If you're unsure, listen to your intuition and fall back.

No Contact is when you leave the person alone and don't come back. No calls, no talking to them _at all._

That includes responding to them or trying to let them down nicely. ***No means no.*** Block and delete them if you have to.

The problem with some people is that they feel like they deserve 'closure' or a reason why, so your wishes to leave them alone have to be explained. They feel like you owe them that.

Yes, it may be nice thing to do but ONLY if you are comfortable with it AND they're open to honest feedback. Not everyone can, especially if their feelings are hurt. Most people don't want to hear that they suck or that their inconsistent behaviors raised red flags and you're saving yourself grief anyway.

If you are honest about how you feel, you have made a boundary and it's disrespectful for them to cross it. If your boundaries aren't clearly defined, people tend to force themselves into your reality for the sake of "knowing why" or trying to change your mind.

The reality is that the way that they feel, isn't your problem. No one is entitled to you without your consent, man or woman. No matter how nice you are, being lax on your boundaries causes problems. Be clear.

The same goes for you.
If the other person wants to leave you, you should honor it. You don't have to drag it out and try to convince them to stay. Respect their boundary, save yourself further heartache and let them go.

Keep them accountable to their decisions in reference to you by honoring their choice to leave, especially if you don't want to be continually hurt by their inconsistent behaviors. Once that sense of security is broken, all you have to go on is that point of reference.

If it hurts you, don't let them come back. "Fixing things" from a place of hurt won't repair anything broken without changes of behavior.

If it's open for discussion to redefine your relationship, make it a conscious choice as to what you will put up with and what's not negotiable. Only the two of you can make those choices.

Honor yourself and make sure you feel respected, validated and valued. If for any reason, the relationship doesn't work for you, leave.

Pussy and babies are not leverage to be used as a toy. Mind games and pussy power to convince someone that they're wrong or to sell them on how right it can be, will get you nowhere because there is no commitment to consistency.

You'll be pouring into an empty cup that can never be filled, stuck with someone with no intentions with you. Who knows what dysfunctional loose ends can transpire from that desperation of holding on to someone that doesn't want to be held on to. It's not worth it. There is always a better situation, even if it's alone.

People can only see you from their depth of understanding and comprehension, so no matter how hard you try, you can't make someone see things your way. Setting a clear and consistent message through your own patterns of behavior of what's acceptable and what's not acceptable to you is the only way. Actions speak louder than words.

"When someone shows you who they are, believe them." Patterns and actions of behavior, not just words. Deeds.

We have this one life here and there are no true 'do overs'. You can make excuses for others or you can make it count for you.

You deserve a quality life that you will enjoy. And only you can do that for yourself. It doesn't depend on anyone else or what anyone else does. It's all you.

I don't care of what statistic comes out or census statements that tell you that there are too many women to one man, it's not true.

Love is everywhere. If you truly work on yourself, that quality individual that you want, will be who you attract. It's always attraction.

Love Façades and "The Competition"

If we have any social media pages, we live our lives on display to a certain degree. We take care to take the best selfies, pictures and videos to share with the world.

We want the world to see us at our best so instead of enjoying the moments at the time, we take a picture to show the world.
The world gets an idea of who we are through what we show in our personal portfolios.

But let's be honest, we're showing only the good parts, the entertaining parts. Wearing the makeup, the clothes, going on the vacations and parties, while staying at the best hotels and houses all on display for all eyes to see.

Social media and reality TV have everyday women buying into a visual perception that the leaders within it can't even attain to.

You see the sadness and the inner conflicts that they have to deal with publicly and the people watching are still subconsciously buying the façade as the standard.

The problem is that even if you don't watch it on TV shows, if we're 'following' or 'subscribing', we are still *watching* them live their lives.

These people live under microscopic scrutiny through the comment sections and op-ed tabloid TV. We know them through their visual presentations and further surmise and deduce who these strangers are by what we see in their pictures and use our own 'detective skills' to scour for inconsistencies and judge their style and character.

We buy the clothes that look like theirs, buy their makeup lines, buy their programs, etc. And we even subscribe to their business models as personalities to mirror the set standard for choices that we make in our own lives. We see this through how many "influencers" are repeating the same model type and same kinds of products. And we buy them.

There's nothing wrong with being a woman as a public figure, just know that public scrutiny is harder than any private angst you'll ever go through. That microscope that you'll be living under will have the world judge you worse than you could ever judge yourself.

So you have to forgive yourself on a regular basis and ignore what others say and think. With the comment sections active on our pages, you can't ignore it, it's in our faces. And because they "know you in their minds", they feel free to critique you.

Looking at ourselves, we get to relive the good times through pictures. The world gets to vicariously live our glamorous life through our camera lens.

It's an ongoing debate that says that it's a fake life. Only scratching the surface. But it is real and it is true. It's just not the whole story.

Reality TV and online shows are just 'microchunks' of what the editor wants us to see. What makes for the best viewing for Clicks, Subscribers and Likes. Then we decide whether or not we see through their lens or make up our own versions of the truth. What we've made up in our minds, that's the real or the fake.

Whether it's shown purely, manufactured or embellished, we still see what they see, live through what they go through and feel free to give our opinions on how they should live their lives or share our viewpoint on what decisions that we would've made if given the same circumstance. We've bought in.

But it's not your life. We use these people to escape and sometimes even compare and sometimes lose touch with own version reality.

Fan favorites go through something negative or positive. We see toxic relationships and friendships and somehow we're emotionally vested in how others relate to each other. Our kids are seeing how their own favorites live their lives the same way and now are determining that "that is real life" and can't sustain a natural human connection or maintain a healthy relationship.

Everything becomes conditional and depends on them buying the façade presented. Paying attention to what the newer generations are viewing is so important because their interpretation of what love and self-love is. It's a scary brainwashing/conditioning and it's very real.

The problem is that now there's a divide amongst women where we are getting the idea of what a 'real woman' is vs, an "insta woman." The reality is, we're all women. We are all living and breathing women. ***We are all real women.*** No matter the sales pitch is, you can't define someone else's *realness*.

You wouldn't want it done to you. So to demean someone because of "embellishments" (surgical or artificial) doesn't mean that the woman is fake, no matter how she chooses to define herself, She's on a journey that we honestly are no a part of.

We change our own hair, clothes and nail length and color because we feel good. If they want to change something permanently for themselves, why do you get to define their "why"? No matter what it took for them to get to the point of permanent changes, it's their walk. Their walk doesn't validate your 'realness' or take away from you in any way.

It's like a block full of pizza shops, all have the same ingredients for the most part, but they also have their own special sauce and spices that differentiates them from the others.

Others form their own tastes based on what is offered; the choices that they feel are available to them. Based on *that*, they'll make their choices, again that has nothing to do with you. You aren't a choice because you aren't an option.

That's why YOU set the standard for what you offer. You have your special sauce, live in your own truth and take care of your own shop. Don't lower yourself to be someone else's choice, don't put yourself in a box that you don't belong in. Don't worry about what other women's offerings are or even that man's preferences are. Mind your own business.

The beauty is that since everyone is vastly different, there are so many choices. You will not be everyone's cup of tea. You may not appeal to the person that you're attracted to. That has to be fine with you. You have no other control over how others feel. That's not a rejection, it's just not your pool.

Contrarily, you wouldn't want just anybody approaching you, especially if you feel like they aren't worthy of you. You want someone that is looking specifically for what *you* have to offer and if you're that person, you'll get what's for you.

There's a division amongst us women have us on different sides of the fence, shaming each other for the differences rather than embracing those differences. Now the men feel like they have to choose based off of our standard for each other.

Again, it's a fake competition that's not real. It's an imaginary contest with multiple winners. Force the results, you'll be the loser. Stay authentic to who you are and what you want. That is why doing the inner work is so important.

No one is 'taking men' from you. That 'lack' philosophy is the biggest reason for division. If he was meant for you, there is nothing in this world that could hold him from you.

Not how someone looks, their hair, sex appeal, dress, pictures, implants could change that. Nothing.

If you stay in our own truth, someone will appear for you. Someone *just for you*. I'm not talking blind hope, it's always attraction. There's someone for you. See the beauty within yourself, let that lead you and that love you seek will find you.

If you're coming from a place of not enough or lack, you will feel the cool breeze of loneliness because you've counted yourself out. Understand that you are whole and that EVERYONE takes the path of least resistance. If you make it hard to love you, no matter how fly you are, people will tap out. You will end up with a lonely or surface relationship that may just have a floating, inconsistent or even worse, non-existent meaning, blaming others for your discontent. You deserve better than that.

Unconditional Love

The same media is dictating how we see the definition of love and relationships. A lot of movies and comedies from the beginning of TV to nowadays are training us what it looks like, with most showing that we have to go through obstacles for the relationships to be "Real" instead of looking within ourselves.

A huge half-truth is that true love is endurance and long suffering through hard times. How can you be in a situation that doesn't serve you at all and you comfortably stay? You can't. Love isn't long-term punishment, where you're at the mercy of someone else's version of love. Don't let anyone tell you otherwise.

Don't get me wrong, things can't be the we want them all of the time. That's when you make a choice to be loved love someone, you let love for that person lead you instead of letting them make the conditions that *they're* comfortable with to define how they'll love you.

You know how you want to be loved. You can define for yourself. You'll know that love isn't a roller coaster of manic ups and downs. It's consistent and true.

Real unconditional love is when you love yourself and allow the other person to love you, *the whole you*; not the conditions they pick and choose in you, to define how and when they'll love you. If that's the case, someone can choose to stop loving you for the same reason. The conditions set forth doesn't suit them anymore so they leave you. That's not love.

Ride or Die vs. For Better or Worse

"Ride or Die" isn't love. Riding the wave of someone else's downward spiral in the name of loyalty isn't fair. Ride or Die is when your companion gets into a predicament that puts themselves in a bad situation and *bad being an understatement.* They expect you to deal with the fallout of their irresponsibility. They want you to become their outlet or solution that may even be almost impossible to deal with the **hope** that time will make the issue go away. But there are no guarantees on how it all affects you.

Their actions reflect that they were not concerned with how these situations would affect you, but they feel like you should ride the wave and cruise the course for the duration with them out of blind loyalty.

The other problem is, they're decided for you what the definition of what your loyalty should be. Never mind your life, it's about them.

*This is not to be confused with **"For Better or Worse"**.* Better or worse refers to a committed relationship that befalls an unexpected circumstance that is beyond the control of either partner and coming together for support is the best way to get through it, no matter how bad things get. Compromises included.

This is why it's important to know who you are in reference to a love equation... If you don't know yourself and really know your partner how can you know if either of you have what it takes to stand the test of time? What are your intentions? What are theirs? Is it defined and understood?

Truly understanding the concept of unconditional love is what equals self-love plus companion love. If you have self-love, then companion love can be just that: Love fueled by companionship that adds to enrichment of your life, not takes away.

If it's not love, it's *unlove*--able. If it's not lovable, save yourself. Living or staying in horrible circumstances (you or your partner) makes you feel like "you don't love me if you leave", it's like *stay here and be miserable with me.* Misery loves company. Real love doesn't do that.

Let your self-love lift you and meet you where you need to be for yourself, lead with love, not conditions and definitely don't settle for less than what you deserve.

You can't control someone else and you can't let someone control you without your permission. You won't be happy like you were meant to be. You shouldn't have to break yourself down to a level that defeats or diminishes you. Martyring yourself diminishes you, like you taking the 'high road' in an unwinnable situation makes you the good person or a victim when things go wrong. Why do that to yourself? You only cheat yourself out of a great self-love and quality connection.

If you're unhappy but settle into a situation expecting it to change, you have settled into an insanity condition because you are expecting things to change while enduring the same behaviors.

That's how you lose yourself and sooner or later when you join your partner in misery, after they've broke you down, is when they cheat or maybe even leave you because you've changed the condition.

You've sunk to their level and you're miserable now and they're not used to 'loving you from that point of view'. They'll tell you that, "You've changed" and they'd be right. When I say the only person that you can change in any situation is you, I mean it.

If you change within the situation, 'good or bad' there's a ripple effect. You've caused the change, so that changes the effect.
If you change, the situation will change, because you've redefined the terms.

If you decide that you want better, do better for yourself. Stay consistent, gain your power and if they decide to roll with your new position, you've helped yourself. But don't let them break you down again. Still maintain your position and stand your ground, not falling back into past behaviors.

If they leave, you have freed yourself. You're allowed to miss them, but move on. Let them stay on the side that they chose. You're free from an unhealthy and conditional existence.

Soul Ties, Twin Flames and Soulmates

After Doug, Melvin and James, I realized that in the ending of those relationships I kept trying harder to be the woman I thought that they wanted and it was never enough because I wasn't true to myself. So how could they give me what I deserved if I was shortcutting myself?

At their time periods, all I knew was that I loved them (in my own way) and wanted them to love me the same way. Sounds cut and dry. Reciprocity is all anyone wants, right?

But I honestly didn't understand what love I needed from them, to give to them, because I didn't understand the love I had for myself. What was my own point of reference?

Well, the less you get from someone you care about, the more we tend to do to compensate for what you're missing. We suffer through the push-pull of anxiety and toxicity when all you have to do is stop and either let him love you or let him go.

When it's uneven, there's not even 50-50 to make one whole couple, because there's no 100% within you (or them) to even start with.

What happens when you're giving yourself less for the sake of being loved?
But most of us didn't learn about that. Generations before us were taught to make it work. To suffer through heartache and pain for the sake of being with our "soulmate, a perceived life partner."

Well, let me be clear. I do believe in soulmates. But I also believe that you will have several soulmates in your lifetime.

A soulmate is someone that feeds your soul, like food. But remember that just like meals don't last forever, sometimes your soulmate can come into your life then go.

Reasons and Seasons, remember?
People sometimes leave scars, some people leave behind lessons and hopefully someone leaves you better off than they way that they met you. Sometimes, they don't leave.

Either way, please don't get hung up on that definition of a person being your once in a lifetime love. Life is too unpredictable for that. Things happen.

Whatever you feel like you've lost, will never be the best you'll ever have. Not even in death. Because until you stop being able to love, there will be more love to be found.

Yes, there are many people who have found 'the one for them', but that's no pressure for you. Your journey is yours alone. There is no need to fill your head with romanticized notions of who you think that person is, was or will be to you. That's when you put those rose colored glasses on again and start seeing what you want to see, to your detriment. It's a vicious cycle that needs to be broken.

What you want from someone and what you need to make it happen has to line-up and it just won't, no matter what you do if you have to force it. If it doesn't work, it won't work. It may not even be meant to be a lifetime connection.

Your true and everlasting forever Mate of your Soul is **_YOU_**.

Everyone has a different mind, heart and a definite way of love _and_ how to love based on what their interpretation is of what love is. You fall in and out of love with yourself all day, everyday. So to place expectations on someone else based your own intricate inconsistencies is unrealistic.

Variety is the spice of life and we're all supposed to be different. People come into our lives to teach us about ourselves. How love is supposed to be for you, how not to be loved and how to allow someone else to love you.

It's trial and error. Natural contrast is the only way to see color in a picture, the darkness and the light, only this is your love picture. That's why _soulmates_ can take many forms: in friendships and romances that last for reasons, seasons and lifetimes.

Love is like a dance. You have a partner, both of you find your rhythm. Lead or be led as you let the dance happen together.

If something happens in life that changes the rhythm, you don't stop dancing altogether. You regroup and after you find your own rhythm again, you can find your rhythm with each other and let the dance move you.

Finding your own rhythm is important in the regroup, even if you have to step back and dance alone for a little while.

In a successful dance, you'll always find your way together with patience and lots of laughs. Knowing your partner's maneuvers can help you two regroup faster, even if the rhythm changes often.

Don't get me wrong, you shouldn't force anything when it's not working out. If you can't find your rhythm together again, even after doing the self-work, sometimes you literally have to stop dancing with each other. Sometimes you even need to find another partner.

Footnote: Some people don't understand that you can't dance the same dance with a new partner. You have to evolve. Learn from your past failures.

Stop looking for your ex in new lovers. Chasing familiar characteristics because it was what you were used to, is still forcing the same you into different relationships. Repeating patterns of behavior based on familiarity is not fair to either of you. There are no shortcuts to love. Know what your intentions are with this new person.

You can't keep going backwards with yourself to that same comfortable familiarity with that old partner mentality. Having that "type" may closing you off from true happiness. When you use your ex as a point of reference, that ghost of *what was* creeps in and steals the joy of *what could be*. That's not fair to you and that new person. Doing the inner work is important.

Now that you know what you want and what you don't want, you now have new tools to work with. If you see that quality of what you don't want in the new person, decide how you'll respond in this new instance.

It can actually help you navigate in this new relationship. It's like choosing different routes in a GPS that takes you to the same place you want to be. You decide what you want to deal with and what you don't; what's worth it, what's not; the joy is in the journey. Trust yourself and you'll find your way.

The Inner work and Trauma

I was raped as a young teen. I was molested as a child. When a woman has those traumas in her past, there are 3 ways she deals with it.

1. On her own.
2. With help.
3. She doesn't deal and she buries it. The secret shame stays with her.

All I knew was that I never felt safe when it came to relationships with men. I wanted to feel safe but I had no definition of what safety was or that I even needed it.

My father was out of our house for most of my life and although I knew that my father loved me, his definition of self-love, healthy relationships and what male roles were supposed to be was skewed.

So I didn't have any idea of what to look for when I picked my first boyfriend, Dave. He was nice and pursued me.

As time went on, he was someone that seemed protective. He had a mother that loved him and several sisters.

Dave was caring and showered me with gifts. He was aggressive but not with me. Until that one Saturday afternoon.

What I did learn, like most young girls, I learned through trial and error and definitely learned what I didn't want.
No matter the length the relationship was, any domestic violence survivors, can tell you that very first time they got hit. We remember it like it was yesterday.

In that moment, we made a defining choice to stay or leave. To endure the abuse or to run for our lives.

Most abusers use abuse as a standard in how they show love, when you accept it, it becomes a condition, something that they'll use in the future as an action against you.

That's why most abusers will manipulate the situation by accusing you of not loving them when you don't accept the condition and want to leave or they'll even say, *I love you but you made me do it.*

When my ex hit me, I had the choice to accept his standard as a woman beater. If I did accept it, it would become the condition he set that hitting me would have been how he defined his love for me in the future. Would this be how he responds to me when he's frustrated or angry?

That person has made the standard, when you agree to the standard by staying, it becomes a condition in your relationship that the victim feels like they have to endure, because the relationship is now defined by the standard of abuse.

Once you get used to living under those conditions, it's hard to see love defined in any other way but negative and aggressive.

It has been said that we are so free that you can choose bondage and that's true.

The welts and bruises appear the same but abuse and bondage are not the same. When you make the *choice* to accept the standard, it becomes a conditional. The scars from each become defined standards in a relationship of power and control but the difference is ***intent.*** Again, bondage and abuse is not the same.

What is in the mind of someone who purposefully inflicts pain? What is in your mind when you choose to accept it and continue in it. In reference to you, you always have to choice to leave/escape the situation.

When you endure abuse in any form, mental, emotional and or physical, it easily gets misconstrued as unconditional love in the other person gaslights you into thinking that warped way that they do.

When you're a child being molested or if you're older and your partner hits or rapes you and tells you that they love you and don't mean to hurt you. Or try to convince you that what you feel isn't pain.

Manipulation is when someone controls or influences you in a way against yourself towards a point that only benefits them.

Gaslighting is when someone psychologically manipulates you into believing that you're crazy to feel what you feel.

Narcissism is extreme selfishness, with the other person's exaggerated view of themselves at the expense of you and your feelings.

All of these forms of abuse are positioned to break you down mentally and emotionally and have the potential to evolve and manifest into physical abuse.

When someone uses what they call unconditional love as *they've* defined it through pain is just misery. Whenever that love makes you feel less than your best self or starts to diminish you in anyway, it's not real love. They can't love you if it's hurting you.

That person knows what your tears look like. They see the fear and hurt in your eyes. You don't have to see physical tears or blood for them to know that you're bleeding.

Time can't ever heal those wounds if you stay with who is inflicting pain on you, it will get worse but your tolerance for the pain will make it feel like it's less. But it isn't. The only thing that will change is the amount of time you wasted at your lowest.

So how do you survive trauma and traumatic relationships?

One day at a time.
You were meant to create a good life for ourselves.

We all know what happens when we are creating in an environment absent of love. We have to learn to get out of it.

You shouldn't be settling or holding onto a relationship at all costs, but you deserve to have a good, healthy love. When you learn to love yourself all over again, YOU will choose the best standard of how someone loves YOU in the future because you've set the standard on how you want your love to feel.

So don't be afraid to leave or be alone for a while. True love will find you once you heal and allow healthy love to flow. But that can only come if you've healed those wounds of the past.

It's like an infected wound. It's painful, throbbing, swollen, full of pus and toxic infection and sometimes that is how some people look going into new relationships, rushing back into love. People do that because they're love starved. They crave some semblance of love.

You take *the wounded you* wherever you go. The same qualities that came out in reaction to being hurt reappear. Why? Because you never let yourself heal.

Being love starved deprived you of the essential healing so we gravitate towards anything that feels good, even defining it as love. Remember, we attract who we are, the best of ourselves and the worst of ourselves. Even if it's the traumatic parts of us that just wants their aggressor to show us mercy. The healing work decides what piece of us gets fed.

Yes, there are people out there that will love the wounded you to safety. OR you could be the same 'angel' for someone else. It is possible that that piece of you attracts your relief.

Be careful of that point of attraction between you and that other person, some 'angels of mercy' are people that love to heal broken souls are also hurt people that find common ground with pain.

You or they become a project for them to fix and it can become conditional if the point of focus is only highlighting your pain instead of working towards your healing or making solutions that lead to a quality relationship for the both of you.

There are so many different ways for love to find you, just make sure that you and that person are benefitting from this love connection. Intentions must be clear.

No matter who loves you, love *outside* yourself heals in a different way. Remember that love needs to start with YOU wanting to lovingly heal yourself. Being conscious of that is how you can meet your lover half way.

It's like when you see a broken limb, there's a cast or splint to keep the bone in place but there has to be you being able to heal so your body does what it's supposed to do and heal. The bone eventually fuses together again and sometimes it feels better than even ever.

That's what your inner work does because the point of trauma has been protected, wasn't been fully utilized for a while and was allowed to heal internally and now able to be used to the best of its ability.

The thing is that when you don't heal properly or rush healing prematurely, those same exposed wounds are still exposed. Hiding behind our traumas, gives us a way not to heal. "He hurt me." It hurts, but we can't want to stay hurt. Guard your heart.

So many of us are so used to being in pain that feeling good even hurts. That's where the expression, "Hurt People, Hurt People." comes from. And being hurt sucks. Life is so much greater than forcing yourself to constantly relive that pain.

That's why people are in therapy for years. I honestly believe that there should be a healing plan in place for therapy. I'm not a doctor to make assessments but I have gone to therapy. It's definitely something that I recommend, especially when you're actively 'doing the inner work'. Knowing that there's something about you that keeps attracting certain people and life choices, yes we may need someone to pull the blanket off of our heads and expose the true wound in order to clean it from infection in order for it to heal properly.

But picking at that scab constantly makes the healing process almost impossible. That therapeutic healing process should include how to reintroduce *yourself to yourself* into powerful aftercare. Giving you the refreshed version of yourself after you're equipped with tools that will help you bring out the best in yourself as well as make for quality connections.

It's like going through a devastating accident and you must go through physical therapy.

Now there are people who don't go to physical therapy and endure pain for years, making them dependent on tools that enable them to function. Problem is, when you don't deal with the problem at hand, it manifests into other problems because your weight is shifted in one direction to compensate for what needs to heal.

It's the same with dealing with traumas. If you rush in and out of relationships or continually lead with your pussy, you end up missing out on feeling with your heart or knowing with your mind if that person is even good for you. Because you're overcompensating for what pain isn't being addressed. That's why we either hurt people or we attract people that hurt us.

Use time and consistent self care to redefine your own intentions for companionship and love, it will help you in the long term.

Some people don't want to heal, they just want to have sex and don't want love. You may not be ready to heal those inner wounds and instant gratification is how you deal. It's your life and we all deal in different ways.

Please make sure that your partners feel the same way. Make sure that there's transparency in what you and your partner are going for.

There's no casual in a true connection and although there have been cases where purely sexual encounters have resulted in love, remember that you take yourself with you wherever you go.

If you don't let your inner wounds heal at some point, heartbreak may result at the end of the line. No one can love you blindly for too long. Both of you have to eventually want the same things in order for it to be built to last, planting real seeds for the future together.

The desire for something real can bring out your being a better you. That desire can heal you too. Don't underestimate the power of desiring a great future, it's an incentive to wanting self-growth that comes from an evolved mindset and perhaps that person can bring out your desire to be a better you.

To stay together, there has to be a constant growth within your relationship and that common ground can carry you. You want that common ground to be full of positive and consistent growth. But you can't be the one to want it for the two of you. That partner has to balance that load by wanting the same thing. Be real with yourself and there will be no confusion.

Baby Mama Drama & Un-Hoeing Yourself

Like so many girls, I was raised to be a wife. Be able to cook, clean and put other's needs above my own. Treasure my chastity from birth and on my wedding night, give the man that I married this gift of my virginity.

As I developed, there became two parts of me. The one that wanted to be a virginal wife and the other part was a young curious woman that wanted to explore my ever-growing womanhood, which is always frowned upon.

The "She's fast" and "She thinks she's grown" are one liner's that stick to girls, and although it never stuck to me, I knew girls that it did stick to. It usually came from people standing in the seat of condemnation because their upbringing was different than theirs.

Thing is, those young ladies grow up and I know those same labels whisper in their own minds.

"We are who we answer to." It's hard when your own mind tells you that that's who you are. "Unlovable" "Hard to love" "Not enough" Now we have evolved and devolved into fractured women that can only love from a place of want.

We become that angry, toxic, misunderstood woman that attracts from that place of wanting to be understood and loved. Wanting someone to fill that hole in our souls, attracting people who seem to fit or fill us.

Either we're giving the energy or they're giving us the human connection, but ends up filling the other while the other ends up depleted.

Where we get wrapped up and end up going from relationship to relationship looking for the connection for someone to fill us the way we try to fill others. You can't meet anyone at that level. That's why a lot of us end up having multiple children, even multiple children with multiple partners.

Then we look at the ultimate symbol of unconditional love: *the love of a child.* An innocent child that needs love and has basic needs that we can reasonably fulfill. They accept what we give, no matter how hard things get, and love us in exchange, right?

Truth is, we can only give what we can and kids always need. Some of us are natural givers and it makes you attract natural takers. Kids are takers. They take the best of us and the worst of us. So we have to be careful of what we give them.

Yes, your kids love you but they have to make their own path eventually and when they become older, whatever tools of self-love that they get from you is from the point of attraction and perspective that you've given them.

The re-direct of the void inside of us into our kids is unrealistic and unfair. It becomes us loving our kids from a place of wanting them to make us their objects of affection.
It becomes the warped condition of us pouring everything into them, expecting our kids will always love us like a transaction expecting a return on our investment.
"If I love them, they'll love me."

That's how we have mothers that make excuses for their children are the ones that overindulge and overcompensate and do their kids (and the world) a huge disservice. The child's inner conflicts mirror yours and if there's a character flaw in your child, it's a glaring reflection, magnified and manifested into how you've raised them.

Holding yourself accountable and detaching yourself from judgments that may mar your objectivity, THAT'S how you show unconditional love for a child. Not what makes you love your kids in the way that's easier for you to love them. Your child learns how to navigate pleasing you instead of learning how to navigate their own feelings in regards to healthy and unhealthy connections.

Our children are given to us for the purpose of us to love and guide them to being great adults, setting them up for success (mentally, emotionally, physically and even spiritually)

"You are only as happy as your saddest child." You can tell who people were internally by how their children deal with their inner demons.

We all have them, if you don't find a way to deal with them now, we raise generations of children that look outside of themselves for that loving connection, guidance and accountability whether it's from you, their future partners, even the streets. It robs them from that true love, which is a healthy sense of self.

It's like dropping a tin pan that we bake cakes in and now's there's a dent. Guess what? All of your cakes will have that same dent.

We give what we can and we owe it to ourselves and our children to want to be better. That can only be done through doing the inner self-love work and can't be done through finding love outside of ourselves.

After my relationship with Doug, I struggled with loneliness and the fear of being a single mother. My mother was a single mother that never had another man after her divorce from my father. It always hurt me to see another man not loving her.

She deserved love and so did I. I definitely didn't want that martyring of a love life for myself.

But here I was: a single mother just like her, struggling with feeling like I was not enough and love starved. There was no way to get to love from the empty way that I was feeling. So I shut my heart off. It was never my feeling like I needed a man, but that I couldn't do both. Be a good mother *and* love someone else in a relationship.

That thinking, attracted Melvin. That relationship verified that mindset. I thought that love would take so much work that would take me away from being a good mother.

But being with James showed me that I didn't mean that I have to be a martyr either. I was still young and deserving of love. He was just not supposed to be my future. We only can love and attract love from our ever-evolving point of attraction.

Depriving yourself of love because of hurt and traumatic experiences isn't the way to go either. Do the inner work, let the wounds heal, the next partner that you attract will be someone that fits what you deserve.

Whether it was depriving myself or overindulging myself, a lot of my choices are not popular and they don't have to be. It's my life, just like your life is yours.

In all that I've been through, put myself through and allowed myself to go through, I've learned that you can't get caught up in what others think of you.

Passing judgment is something humans do. It's easy for someone else to look in your garden and point out the weeds. I always say, how someone feels about you is none of your business. People like to hold you to what they think you are, without truly even knowing their own wants and needs... but they know all about yours.

It's hard to trust women that don't trust each other and then have daughters. How can that work? How can you show a future woman how to love herself under the guise of not trusting a part of yourself?

The biggest piece of hypocritical behavior is the premise is that after making recurring pussy decisions that people question your character for, you literally do a 180 degree turnaround and move on with your life in a monogamous relationship, even a marriage.

How dare *you* become a wife? How dare *you* find love? How dare someone 'wife' *you*? After everything you've done, how can he ignore your "track record"? "Can't turn a hoe into a housewife." and other ignorant ideologies.

Most people live in glass houses and the thought of such a woman is an enigma whereas men in the same position are lauded and applauded for their maturity. Oh the double standard!

I will always say this: Although people tend to not let you forget your past, you have every right to be another or even the better version of yourself at *any time*.

We see ourselves in each other, good, bad and ugly. The love and hate within ourselves, those qualities that we either embrace or those that we admire. All of that comparing against our own ideals is the way we can identify traits in others.

Just remember that the pointing finger that's aimed at someone else's life or situation may be something that we really need to look at within ourselves. Maybe there's a deep-rooted reason we feel the way that we feel. But is how they live their own lives still your business? You have to heal from what they symbolize or it will consume you and redefine your attraction.

Meanwhile, there are women who've changed their lives while the public chooses to hold them in their own place of comfortability, while continuing to hold you to what they perceive you to be, they're used to you having inner struggles and that's what makes them comfortable to deal with you from.

It takes a strong person to move on from a notable "low point" in their life instead of letting people hold you there. Life is too good and you are supposed to grow and evolve through trail and error.

Imagine how fruits and vegetables would taste if we took them in the form that they started in instead of letting them blossom. There would definitely not be any such thing as juicy and delicious. We'd adapt to the idea of what it tastes like but definitely not enjoy it if it wasn't allowed to mature and evolve.

With time, being hard and bitter can turn soft and sweet.

You need no one's permission to change. You don't have to be the same person from 20 years, last year or even an hour ago.
And NO ONE has the right to hold you there. And that goes for anyone else.

When you allow yourself to be who you want to be and give yourself the life that you deserve, the right people will be happy for you. But be warned again, most people aren't comfortable with change so some will be mean and downright disrespectful.

We see it all of the time with female celebrities on social media, but don't let it change your course. Stay strong and define your life on your own terms.
You deserve to love, be loved and have a great life to be enjoyed. Don't let anyone hold you to your past.

Contrarily, some people will always be who they are and that's fine too. Let them be. If you cross paths with them or if they're a constant in your life, you may have to let them go.

If people you love are holding you to their level of understanding and it's drowning your chances for a happy life, let yourself off the hook and move on. How they feel about you is none of your business, unless you make it. Love yourself to know the difference.

However telling and self-explanatory, I wouldn't call it an un-hoe-ing, I'd call it a coronation of sorts, switching up and wearing your crown. Now, you've found a way for you to stop letting your pussy think for you, for you to make a conscious decision to live your life on terms that you're proud of.

The terminology behind being a hoe needs to be defined the way you want to define it. No one has the right to define your sexuality for you. Hoes are garden tools. You are a woman. A woman that is evolving into the woman she will be eventually. This is a temporary period in your life that shouldn't define you. You're learning, so learn. Like time, keep moving forward.

Remember that your journey to self is NEVER over. You will always grow, evolve and live to tell the tale, no matter who you choose to be with.

Love who you want, be with who you want and define your own terms of happiness, as long as *you are* mentally and emotionally happy. Not settling, not in need or in want of more. Definitely not delusional about your own reality, but genuinely happy with who you are in every scenario. That's a real peace of mind.

Think of going on a road and you hit a dead-end. When you look closer, you see another rocky road that looks really dangerous, but it's still a path. What do you choose? Do you push your way "through" the dead end?

A lot of people decide to take the hard path when they don't even consider the option of completely turning around and finding a different journey. Us thinking that the only choice off of the dead end is going the hard way is baffling.

But yet we do it all of the time. We choose the hard way like life and love is supposed to be hard.

If that path that you've gone down ends up being a dead-end, whether with self or in a relationship with nothing in it for you to grow and be a better version of yourself as well as growing & being better together, your decision is simple, get off the road and turn around.

They'll be better off and so will you.

If you decide that the only path is the dangerous road, remember that unless you have the gear to endure whatever comes from taking the dangerous road, it's futile.

That superwoman, *"Can do"* or *"We'll get through this"* attitude will only wear out our tires on that road. What is truly in it for you? The martyrdom badge that *"You tried?"*

Going down the road in the first place was your try. Pushing boundaries that aren't good for you do not serve you. Do yourself a favor and re-evaluate the journey that you're embarking on, whether it's in life or in love.

Remember that it's always up to you to change your life. Always shift up.

If it's meant to be, they'll catch up on the road that you've chosen for yourself, not one that you've settled into for them.

If not, hopefully you'll learn the lesson that you were meant to learn that will eventually bring you closer to the love that you deserve.

Thinking With My
Doing The Work...

In wanting to attract your new partner, you should have a list of qualities in yourself that match what you want in that potential mate.

I want to be with a smart, kind and handsome man. Well, Do I feel smart? Am I kind? Do I take pride in my appearance? Why are these qualities important to me?

When someone says that you have unrealistic expectations, it's because the qualities that you may want in someone else, may not be qualities that you yourself embody.

It's time to be honest with YOURSELF.

Do you want children? If you have children, do you want more? If the person that you're interested in doesn't want children, then you being a parent means that this person may not be ideal as your potential mate. There's a point in the beginning of a connection when you have the opportunity to be honest.

It's better to take the chance and be told no because of your honesty instead of the person that gets the yes under false pretenses. Dishonesty sets everyone up for disappointment.

If you're still in any form of a relationship, you are not in any position to pursue ANYONE. If you choose to opt for an open relationship, make sure that ALL PARTIES involved have a say. Respectful relationships have transparency. If you can't handle that, you need to reevaluate how you function in relation to other people.

If you have no intentions of being in a relationship, let that be known. You can find someone that has the same ideals and may not want a relationship, just like you.

Be consistent. If that's what you want, don't change that. You do yourself an injustice with being a part of a bait and switch. If someone changes the dynamic that you both intended, then you have to decide if those conditions are for you. *You set the standard.*

Please don't settle for the sake of not being lonely. If this person doesn't embody what's important to you, even if they're perfect in ever other way, they aren't for you.

There is someone for everyone. There is no shortage, no lack of partners in this life. When you're truly ready, you'll have the opportunity to be honest. If it doesn't fit, don't force it, simply walk away and respect the other person's choice to walk away from you.

Being good on paper, swept up in lust or love at first sight mean absolutely nothing if the TWO OF YOU aren't ready for each other. Nothing.

We've all heard about doing a puzzle. The "big picture" is supposed to be a certain way, there's a proper place for all of the pieces. We all know about when you start in the beginning, the picture is blurry and the pieces are everywhere.

You find pieces of the puzzle by seeing the similarities.

They'll be times when things don't belong together, because just because it can "fit", doesn't mean it belongs in the place you put it.

Who you are in reference to the puzzle components, you'll find the corresponding pieces that belong. That makes the big picture. The thing about people is that as we grow and evolve, our own puzzles are never done. The beauty of companionship is the coming together to figure out new puzzles together, while each other figures out their own at the same time.

Even after you do the work, you may still attract someone that may not be good for you. *That's* part of the lesson.

- Know when to close the door. You don't have to go thru it to know it's not good for you.

- Look for the value in your past relationships and forgive yourself.

- Think of what you'd love to have as a quality in someone else, and meet yourself there.

- Do what's required within to meet yourself there.

- And when you find those qualities in that special someone, relax into love. Explore, have fun and take your time.

If that person turns out not to be the one, rinse and repeat the steps. Sounds simple, right?

When you're not self-aware,
You'll keep crashing and burning in situations that you feel like you have no control in.

If you are with someone and they leave, they were teaching us something.

Take the lesson or the same pattern of men will continue in your experiences. Holding on to an idea of what their love meant for the sake of habit is unfair to you. Let them go. It may feel impossible at the time, but see the blessing in the desertion.

After my first boyfriend, I subconsciously thought that all men cheat. So I manifested a cheater. The things you're afraid of come and stick to you like flies to your windshield.

Then there were the people, friends and lovers that I allowed into my life knowing that they added absolutely nothing to the quality of my life.

Relationships are how you relate to someone.

Ask yourself was there a theme to that relationship? Was I always making apologies for who I was? Was I my best self? How did I feel about myself? What made me feel that way?

Casting blame robs you of a chance of self-accountability and the opportunity to make change. Take off the rose colored glasses and truly look at yourself in your past relationships. Decide that you don't want to settle in roles that you aren't comfortable with anymore.

Looking back, if I was mentally, emotionally, physically and even spiritually at my best at that time, would I have even *chose* him again? Of course not! And I didn't have to be with him again to know that.

You can't get your precious time or energy back so don't waste your time with regrets and closure.

Closure is a lie.

1) You're just torturing yourself by bringing up the past to get a sorry that someone else doesn't want to give or may not even be ready to admit and give.

And 2) Don't let someone rip the bandage off to make you relive painful memories to make themselves feel better.

The true closure is: **Close Your Door.**

Run and don't look back. Even with having children that resulted from these painful relationships, be grateful for the beautiful gifts and be grateful that the sun always shines after a storm. Appreciate the newfound freedom from the self-torture you endured in the name of love.

That's why you have to always be the best version of ourselves. Work on ourselves at all times.

When carrying a heavy load on a farm, a farmer puts 2 of the same kind of animal that can carry the evenly distributed weight. If the load is too heavy on one side, the cart can tip and they can lose the load, even causing injury to one of the animals.

Sometimes we are two people that are attached that for whatever reason, but clearly shouldn't be together.

One of them ends up carrying the brunt of the burdens or does the heavy lifting in the relationship. Is that fair? When would it ever be equal? Does the other person that's lacking in the relationship actually want to ever rise to the occasion and be the person they need to be to have the connection that they both deserve?

A healthy give and take, I water you, you water me is a reciprocity that feeds both partners.

Whether or not I chose them from heart, mind or lust, I definitely didn't choose them from the best part of myself, only pieces of myself.

I know who I am *now*. I know what appeals to my mind, the type of person that I could love and if those are all on the same page, my pussy will be happy.

Thinking _with_ your pussy is the best thing you could do for yourself. No more unfinished-self decisions. No more self-doubt and defeating notions about yourself in reference to love. Your heart and mind are all involved and knowing with certainty what's best for you is the order of the day.

But it has to be all _about you first_. Build your strength. Find inner peace. Start that business. Do everything that you've ever wanted to do. Loving yourself is the real upgrade. No outside force can do that for you. You have to do that for you.

Start by asking yourself: Who am I? Who do I want to be? Am I that person? What do I need to do to get to be that person?

Then you can do the honest work with yourself, become who you want to be and then you ask, what qualities do I want in a companion that would help me maintain my happiness?

If and when you attract a future partner, you will be self-loved and ready for the outer love you deserve.

For the first time, I was alone but not lonely. I was fine with having a lover or not and it all depended on me and my needs. I treated myself well all of the time and never accepted less than what I felt I deserved. I used my power of choice. My own satisfaction comes first, then I can teach others how to treat me.

My life, my happiness was paramount and made my paths clear. Always treat yourself better and you will have better.

My passion increased, I vibrated higher, my propensity to love intensified and it invigorated me.

When we know how to love ourselves, we pick better, we love better and are able to show others how to love us.

Always remember, the quality of our lives depends on us and only us.

THANK YOU

First, I would love to thank my son Bam for being my constant inspiration to be the best mom that he deserves. I love my niece Iana that makes me aware that love always unfolds and because of our unconditional bond, our love grows stronger and stronger.

You munchkins make me want to be bigger and better.

Then I want to thank myself.

Loving myself through all of my inner battles and outer triumphs is the best thing I could ever keep doing for myself. My inner work is never done and I expect to give and receive the same love and acceptance from my future.

ABOUT THE AUTHOR

Birdie Chesson is the Author and Illustrator and Publisher to all of her many books.
She also teaches others how to write their own books through her coaching workshops and seminars with over 20 years of experience as a public figure.
She is the mother of a son, Bam.

To find out more about her, visit: www.BirdieChesson.com

Are you interested in booking a Workshop, Seminar or Conference with Birdie Chesson?

Most Popular Workshops:
- Momtrepreneurs
- Girl Power
- Entrepreneur Love
- Family Talk
- Let's Write a Book!

Birdie Chesson can also insert your mission statement within her message for your group or organization.

Interested in having Birdie host your next event? Would you like coaching? For more information visit, BookCoachBirdie.com

Email Birdie at Hello@BirdieChesson.com

Thank you for reading a book by:

Please feel free to enjoy her other publications:

- Entrepreneur Love
- Saggy Boobs, Stretch Marks & Saddlebags
- Let's Write a Book!

And her Children's Book Series'
- Stickboy & Cookie
- "Talk to Me"

Visit: MissBirdiesBooks.com
Facebook.com/MLFChronicles